Changed

Autobiography of
Tom Cantor

2020

Dedicated to the one who changed me.

Preface

Many of us have dark secrets that we want to conceal from others. We all share the same tendency to hide those secrets and run away from those realities when they threaten our self-image. This brings serious consequences. We become dishonest with ourselves and less real. These consequences prevent the real us from getting close to others. Whether admitted or not, the truth is that a secret makes a person keep his distance from others out of fear that they will find out what is hidden. Conversely, when a person courageously and humbly decides to expose the truth that person becomes real to both himself and others.

The purpose of this book is to break the damaging cycle of secrets that cause dishonesty and distance. For fifty years I have not been transparent nor real. I deliberately kept a dark secret that was a threat to my reputation and self-image. Months before our marriage, I learned from my wife that she had been raped and was pregnant. I was crushed, shattered and devastated. In particular, wanting to protect myself, I kept this a secret for over fifty years. During those five decades, hiding this dark secret robbed me of the freedom to be myself, creating a distance between me and others. With this book, I have made the decision for the first time in fifty years to embrace the transparency and reality that I hid from myself and others. In this fifty-year journey, I have come to understand how burdensome and imprisoning it is to run away from the truth. Through this book, it is my desire to help others do what I had to do: become a real person who is transparent and close to others.

Table of Contents

Part 1: Broken

"I am Jewish"

My name is Tom Cantor. I am founder and president of Scantibodies Laboratory – a company which grew from my tiny single-car garage and only $130 investment in 1976 to an 800 team-member company with world-wide operations. I would like to tell you how I was changed!

With both my parents Jewish, I was born into a typical Los Angeles Jewish community. Being the grandson of an orthodox Rabbi from the Lithuanian Kantorovich Rabbinical line, religion was in my family. In spite of my grandfather Cantor/Rabbi's influence, I grew up as a secular Jew attending Reformed and Conservative synagogues not by my choice but because my parents said I had to.

Temple Emanuel in Beverly Hills

Sinai Temple in Los Angeles

My father was a prominent Beverly Hills obstetrician/gynecologist known for developing a stress incontinence female surgical technique. My mother worked for the Henry Wilson talent agency that represented well-known actors such as Rock Hudson, Troy Donahue and Tab Hunter. As successful as they were professionally, my mom and dad were not good at marriage; they got divorced when I was one year old. My father was married five times and my mother, three times.

Being Jewish defined me: a moyle (one who performs the Jewish covenant of circumcision) circumcised me when I was eight days old; I regularly attended synagogue growing up; participated in the major Jewish holidays; and was enrolled in Hebrew day school. This early exposure to being Jewish gave me some passing thought as to whether or not God really existed. But, the strong culture of Judaism overshadowed that question. Judaism for me was not spiritual/ religious, it was just a heritage.

Celebrating the Jewish holidays was an integral part of our family. During the Passover celebration we gathered in a home to hear again and again how the Egyptians had tried to exterminate the Jews and how God sent Moses to deliver the Jews from Egypt. Every year we went to synagogue for Rosh Hashanah (New Year) and Yom Kippur (Day of Atonement) High Holiday services.

On Yom Kippur we were reminded that all of our past year's sins or everything we did wrong would be atoned for. The slate would be wiped clean. I used to wonder how bad sins could really be if they could be so easily wiped clean every year.

As I sat in the synagogue on Yom Kippur, I looked around and wondered what was wrong with all of us that we all kept sinning every year. How could I be sure that all of the past year's sins were adequately recalled so they could all be atoned for?

Sitting all day on those uncomfortable, hard wooden benches, I worried. What if, in my memory, I whitewashed a sin and did not confess it, would I still be forgiven? How could I know if I was being honest enough to admit all of my sins? Was I being sincere enough when I confessed my sins so I would not face judgment? What would happen if I was not sincere enough? I knew I had to return every year on Yom Kippur, because I was the rebellious kid who always was in trouble. For me, Yom Kippur High Holiday might as well have been called, "Day of Tom Cantor Sin Atonement" High Holiday.

My sins were so many that when the call came in the Yom Kippur service to remember them, I really didn't know where to start. As I attempted to recall each of my sins I was disturbed. But I tried.

Urban Military Academy

When I was seven years old, I was sent to the Urban Military Academy in West Los Angeles. Jewish families never send their kids to military school. But my parents felt they had no choice. In my sharply pressed military uniform I did not look like the trouble-maker I was.

Trouble Maker in Disguise

On the very first day of my orientation in military school they called my attention to the fire alarm. I was told in no uncertain terms never to touch it. Rebellious by nature, I could not resist that challenge. Every time I passed that fire alarm my hand went up. It felt so good to touch it. One day my touch dislodged the loose glass. I could not believe it when I saw the glass fall out and shatter on the floor. Then came that piercing alarm that was heard throughout the school. The whole school shut down and hundreds of students had to evacuate. My fellow class mates were quick to point at me as the guilty one. There was no place for me to hide. My immediate punishment was to stand with arms stretched out holding a rifle for hours. That ended my military career as at the age of eight I received a dishonorable discharge and was expelled from the Urban Military Academy. The only option left for me was to be enrolled in the public school system: West Hollywood Grammar School and Emerson Junior High School and only one year at University High School, because my father decided to send me to a boarding school.

By the time I was fifteen, I wanted a stable home life which I never had. I bounced between my mother's house and my father's house. The problem was that I just could not get along with either my most recent stepmother or my most recent stepfather. There was really no place for me to live anymore, no home for me to belong to. I was lost!

"Switzerland Will Clean Him"

One day I went to the Hughes Grocery store in Santa Monica which had record albums. I selected fifteen albums and threw them in one of the empty boxes next to the cashier. I left the store and then returned and asked the cashier if I could take an empty box. I took the box that had the albums. As soon as I walked out the front door with the "empty box" in my hand the police were waiting to hand cuff me. At the police station I was booked for shop lifting. My Dad was both angry and embarrassed when he arrived at the police station. But, he managed to convince the officer-in-charge to have my charges dropped and my record expunged with the promise I would receive psychological help.

That same night my father wanted to get a professional to find out what was wrong with me. He drove me to the office of his friend, a prominent UCLA psychology professor. According to his friend's professional evaluation, I was really a good kid. (I knew he was wrong.) He told my Dad that the problem was that the Los Angeles environment had corrupted my good nature.

My Dad and his friend decided that I should be sent to the French-speaking Monte Rosa boarding school on Lake Geneva at the foot of the clean snowy Swiss Alps in Montreux, Switzerland. They had concluded that Switzerland would "clean" me. It was going to be the clean Swiss environment that would purify my soul of the moral pollution of Los Angeles. (I knew they were wrong again; the real issue had always been me. After all, my father called me "Mazik" meaning "destroyer.")

One cold evening, I boarded the all-night flight from Los Angeles to Kennedy Airport in New York City.

Los Angeles International Airport in 1965

From there I was to sail by ship crossing the Atlantic Ocean to Europe. This would be a new adventure for me. I had never been overseas.

Arriving early the next morning, I reported to the HMS Queen Mary to drop off my trunk with the porter. My trunk mainly contained my prized

Motown record albums. I had seven hours before the ship left. So, I made off for the Big Apple. It felt so good to be free from my parents. I got back to the ship on time. I walked up the steep gangway to board the Queen Mary. As my feet landed on the deck of the ship, I felt alone. Embarking on this new experience and facing the unknown at the age of fifteen, I was overwhelmed by a deep sense of fear and yearning to belong.

As the ship slowly pulled away from its mooring, all the passengers rushed to the stern of the boat to wave, with white handkerchiefs, their goodbyes to loved ones ashore who also waved with white handkerchiefs. I thought I was the only one on the Queen Mary that did not have someone on the dock with a white handkerchief to wave goodbye to me.

The HMS Queen Mary in New York Harbor

The feeling of isolation grew. I slowly made my way to my cabin. Knowing I could not spend the whole voyage huddled and isolated in my cabin, I ventured out. I met four other students going to the same school and all were attractive girls. Things were looking up!

The ship arrived in Le Havre, France and all of us students took a train to Switzerland. On the train and in a new environment, my old rebellious nature again took over. I was so loud and annoying to the passengers around me that the Swiss Police had to come and put me under control. One of them picked me up by the ear and told me that I was a guest in their country and they could throw me out of their country at any time. With that said I managed to behave for the rest of the train trip.

Finally, the train arrived in the Montreux station. I checked in at the Monte Rosa Boarding school and began to settle down.

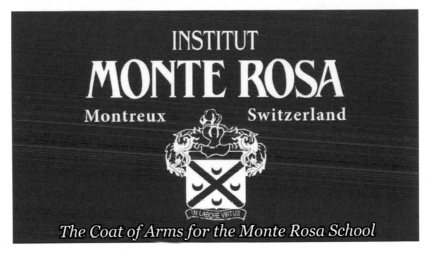

The Coat of Arms for the Monte Rosa School

The Front of the Monte Rosa School (just inside and to the left of the door was the stone staircase)

Behind the Monte Rosa School

Montreux, Switzerland

Monte Rosa School on Lake Geneva

With what happened on the train and what was going to happen, it became obvious that the "corrupt" Los Angeles environment had never been my issue. It was me. Seven weeks after I arrived in Montreux the local police arrested me for being drunk and fighting in the streets. They dragged me back to the school in shame. There I was again, seven years after being expelled from a military school, now being expelled from a boarding school in Switzerland. The head-master of the school told me that the next morning they would drive me to Geneva and place me on a flight back to Los Angeles and that my father was going to pick me up in Los Angeles. One thing I knew was that I did not want to be on that flight the next day back to Los Angeles. I had to do something to have that flight leave without me on board.

That night before the flight home I came up with a plan. Back in my room I fumbled through my stuff and found a pack of razor blades. I stuffed them deep into my back pocket. Then, I waited for everyone to be seated at dinner so that the hallways were empty. (When the fire alarm went off in military school there were witnesses that were quick to blame me. This time I made sure there would be no witnesses.) I stood at the top of the stairs and threw my books down the staircase and then I threw myself and rolled down the long stone staircase, screaming as I hit each of the stone steps. I laid at the bottom of the stairs like a crumpled piece of paper screaming and clutching my back over my kidney.

The ambulance was called. I was put on a stretcher and from that stretcher was the last time I saw the inside of the Monte Rosa Boarding school. At the Montreux Hospital I told the doctor that I had pain in my kidney. The nurse gave me a urine container and left the room to give me some privacy. That gave me the golden opportunity I was waiting for. I urinated into the container and reached into my back pocket for the razor blades. I took out one blade and positioned my index finger over the urine sample. I held my breath and cut the tip of my finger. I watched the red blood drip onto the yellow urine. I swirled the mixture. The nurse knocked on the door and I handed her the red urine sample.

I was told that I had injured my kidney and had to remain in the hospital. The finger cutting plan had worked. The next day I was watching the clock when the flight in Geneva, bound for Los Angeles, took off without me on board. The problem was that I had not thought what I should do in the hospital after the plane left without me. So, I just kept on cutting another finger every time they asked for a new urine sample. Then came the next challenge. Just as I was starting to run out of fresh finger-tips to cut, a physician came to my room and told me that surgery was being scheduled to repair my damaged kidney. I panicked when I thought of a surgeon using his scalpel to cut me open. I had a sudden and miraculous recovery. The next urine sample I handed to the nurse was completely clear. They returned and told me that surgery was not necessary. Another bullet dodged.

Now, the hospital was getting ready to discharge me, but I was expelled and could not return to the Monte Rosa boarding school. I did not have the record that made me a desirable student to be accepted by a new boarding school. From Los Angeles my father was able to find a new boarding school that was willing to take me. The French-speaking all boys' school, the Lycée Jaccard, was just down the road, also along Lake Geneva in Lausanne, Switzerland. I entered the school for a fresh new start. This time I determined that I was not going to be expelled again.

Lycée Jaccard with its blue-roofed boat house

The front door of the Lycée Jaccard

The back of Lycée Jaccard on Lake Geneva

The classroom building of Lycée Jaccard

Over the next two years at the Lycée Jaccard, I wanted to come home for the summers, but my parents wanted to leave me in Europe. They were too busy with their lives to even visit me in Europe. So, while the other students went home for the summers I felt abandoned. That made Switzerland feel all the more cold to me. I was an outcast. I wanted to feel that I was wanted. I wanted a place to belong that was not an institutional boarding school.

"I am Dirty"

During the summer breaks from school I left the cold institution of the Lycée Jaccard boarding school and travelled all over Europe by train, boat and hitchhiking. What I was looking for was that person who wanted me and who I could belong to. During those trips my sexuality woke up. I hoped that sexual intimacy would fill my emptiness and bring me peace and happiness. I turned to women looking for comfort and love. But, the women I turned to were not looking for love, they were only looking for a new passing excitement. Those sexual encounters not only left me feeling emptier, but, worse, they made me feel filthy inside. I FELT DIRTY INSIDE! I was looking for love with all the wrong women. Those relationships failed to deliver love, but they did leave me with a very distinct knowledge that I was sexually defiled. I felt ashamed, guilty and tormented by an inner sense that I was not clean.

Now my problem was how I would get morally cleansed. The feeling of being morally dirty was so strong that one night I walked into the dorm shower with a bar of white soap and washed and washed and washed for two hours trying, to scrub myself clean. I left that long shower feeling as dirty inside as I did when I went in. I could not clean out the memories of my sexual experiences.

Those memories left me feeling guilty and ashamed. I graduated from the Lycée Jaccard with not just a high school degree, but with a dirty heart. I needed to find a way to get cleansed from my sexual defilement.

"Cheryl will Cleanse me"

Graduating from the Lycée Jaccard at the age of seventeen I was faced with the decision of which University to attend. The year was 1968, the middle of the LSD-fueled sexual revolution. Los Angeles looked terrifying. I wanted a place where I could escape my feeling of guilt and shame. With my relatives living just 35 miles away in Cincinnati, Miami University in Oxford, Ohio looked perfect.

Away from Europe and now in Ohio the foul sexual memories continued to hound me. What made it all worse was the feeling that I was isolated and had no one to belong to! At school I had a dorm room with no roommates. One night I was in my dimly-lit dorm room when I hit bottom. I was so depressed that I thought that the only way out was suicide. That scared me. I thought there must be another way out of being trapped by memories that made me feel dirty. I concluded that if moral defilement and a need to belong were my problems, then I needed to find a girl that was different from the women I encountered in Europe. I decided that I needed to find the girl who was wholesome and pure who I could belong to and who could make me feel "clean." My goal was to find a clean girl that could give me pure affection, tenderness and care.

That night I left my dorm room and went to the basement of the university library. I was on the hunt for that serious student who I could engage in conversation and develop a close relationship with. I made my way to the private student study rooms that were all lined up in a row. Each door to the rooms had a square window that I could look into. A technician piped into each room the music that each student wanted to listen to while studying. I stood at the head of the row of rooms and looked at those windows and said, "Perfect! Window shopping!" I slowly made my way glancing into one window after the next. Finally, I found her. There she sat. She was pretty with blonde hair and blue eyes. She was modestly dressed. She looked pure and wholesome to me. Little did I know that in sixteen short months that girl would be my wife.

I made my move. I put on a sheepish face. I gently knocked on the door and with self-assurance slowly opened it. She curiously looked up at me. I said, "Excuse me, I want to listen to the same music you are listening to, but there are no free booths available. Would you mind if I shared this room with you?" (Which of course was not true because there were free booths available.) Appearing to be sorry that there were no booths available, she agreed. I sat down across from her. The music was very strange. Motown music it was not. Smiling and somewhat pleased, she immediately asked me, "So, why are you also interested in African tribal music?" I did not know anything about African tribal music. I dodged her question and asked her what her name was and where she was from.

Her name was Cheryl and she was from Akron, Ohio. I saw she was studying French, I told her that I had just graduated from a French-speaking high school in Switzerland. I asked her if she would like to speak some French to me so

I could evaluate her French accent. She tried to converse in French. Seeing an opportunity to spend time with her I told her that her accent was terrible and that I could help her with her accent, even though I knew I had a terrible Swiss accent. She accepted my offer. I found the "friend" I needed.

I started talking about my family, I told her that my grandfather was an Orthodox Rabbi. She was surprised. She looked closely at me and said, "You are Jewish?" I told her that I was. She told me that she was not Jewish, but that she was raised in a Jewish community and that she had many Jewish friends. She went on to tell me that she loved the Jewish people. That sounded ridiculous to me that anyone who was not Jewish would love the Jewish people. So, I asked her why. She told me that her favorite book was written by Jewish people and that her favorite person was Jewish. I asked her which book it was and who the Jewish person was that she was talking about. She lifted a large well-worn leather-covered book. It was the Bible. She went on to explain that her favorite person was Jesus Christ who was also Jewish. All I thought was, "I hope I become her favorite person."

The more she talked the more I admired her as someone beautiful not only on the outside, but also inside. Clearly Cheryl was the opposite of me. She was better than me; she was pure and wholesome. She was just the person I was looking for.

We Fell in Love

The more I got to know Cheryl, the more I loved everything about her. I loved the way she looked and thought and expressed herself. We both wanted to spend time with each other. We talked on the phone for hours. Cheryl told me that she had pushed her bed across the room next to the wall phone to make it easier for her to spend hours on the phone with me. To have more time with her, I convinced her that her daily schedule was unorganized. Scheming, I offered to mesh our two class schedules together so that we shared all our common free times with each other. In short, I took over her schedule. She never objected.

My thoughts were preoccupied with Cheryl and hers with me. Cheryl shared that whenever she called home to talk with her mother, all she talked about was me. Her mother got concerned and warned her, "Cheryl, don't lose your head over this boy." However, that warning fell on deaf ears. Our love was growing stronger and stronger each day. Desiring to spend our lives together, we began to talk about marriage.

As a matter of fact, we could not have been more opposite. I was the unstable, insecure, defiled world-traveler. She was the stable, sheltered, mid-western wholesome, pure girl. As my relationship with Cheryl continued to blossom so blossomed a new hope in me that Cheryl was my path to cleansing. She had peace in her soul that I envied.

She had an inner life of light that I wanted. Cheryl was all that I needed. I had hoped to extract a cleansing nectar of life from Cheryl. I looked at her as my "liberator." Madly in love our bond to each other was unbreakable.

"She is not Jewish!"
(My Father)

It was now my turn to share with my father my new-found love. That summer when I returned home from Miami University, I told my father that I had met a girl. Quickly my father turned to me with one question, "Is she Jewish?" My father did not want to know anything else about her unless she was Jewish. When I said that she was not Jewish, my father was livid. He asked why I did not follow his instructions to join the Hillel campus organization to find a Jewish girl. I did not tell him that it was too late. I had already found the love of my life, a non-Jewish girl, Cheryl.

Now, my father was determined to dislodge this non-Jewish girl from my heart. To forcefully drive a wedge between Cheryl and me, he called his friend, Dr. Herb Newman, to come with us on a five-hour drive to Las Vegas. I had no choice, but to go on the drive. My father and Dr. Newman sat in the front seat and I sat alone in the back seat for what became an intense indoctrination. On the road and trapped in the car, I was strongly lectured that the history of the Jewish people is a history of the Gentiles murdering the Jewish people. They told me that no Gentile could be trusted. They rehearsed over and over again how the Nazis murdered the Jews and how all the Nazis were Christians. (I thought to myself, "Cheryl does not look like a Nazi to me.") When we reached Las Vegas they had actually accomplished with me just the opposite. I chose Cheryl. They finished their lecture with an order to me to break the relationship with Cheryl. That absolute order made my mind flash back to when I was eight years old in military school. I thought of that other absolute order to not touch the fire alarm and how I took it as a challenge to do the opposite. I now took this new order to break up with Cheryl as a challenge to do just the opposite.

My father was convinced that he had succeeded in persuading me to obey his order to cut the tie. And his parting words were, "Cheryl is not Jewish!" (Little did my father know that the depth and the strength of my commitment and love for Cheryl was unstoppable. My heart dictated to me to defy my father's order to leave Cheryl. I could not and would not!)

"We are not Jewish!"
(Cheryl's Mother)

I returned to Miami University and spent a holiday with Cheryl at her parents' house in Akron. When Cheryl's parents saw that Cheryl and I were serious about each other, their attitude towards me changed for the worse. According to Cheryl, her mother had taken her aside and told her that their family was not Jewish and that Cheryl was not Jewish. Her mother warned her that a mixed marriage was destined for trouble. Her mother told her that a major problem was going to be which faith the children would be raised in. She said that I would insist that the children be raised Jewish instead of Christian. Like my father, her parents objected that Cheryl and I were not compatible. Her mother's words were, "We are not Jewish!" (Little did her mother know that the depth and the strength of Cheryl's commitment and love for me was unstoppable. Her heart dictated that she defy her parent's order to leave me. She could not and would not!)

"Will You Marry Me?"

I was nineteen years old and Cheryl was twenty-two when I made the second most important decision in my life. She had already graduated in December 1969 and, unlike me, would not be returning to Miami University. She had moved back home to Akron, 250 miles away from Oxford, Ohio. I could not bear the thought of that distance between us. With time running out, it seemed to me it was now or never. So, at 2:00 am in the morning in her parents' house I asked her, "Will you marry me?" Cheryl said, "Yes."

Dashed Expectation

When Cheryl said, "Yes" that she would marry me, that was the happiest moment in my life. I was so full of joy and hope for the future. At last, a union with her was going to liberate me from my own guilt, shame and despair. I was finally going to be clean! But, I could never have imagined what was to come next. From the height of great expectation, I fell to the depths of despair. In the same breath when she said "Yes," to my proposal, she gave me devastating news. With her head bowed and with tears running down her face she told me that she had been raped and was now pregnant.

Earlier that summer when I was in California, Cheryl, as an International Studies major, decided to travel throughout Europe with her best friend, Linda Aidala and another girlfriend. Cheryl never planned to travel alone, vulnerable and unprotected. However, shortly after arriving in Europe, Linda and the other girlfriend decided to change their plans and go to Spain where Linda had been an exchange student. Not having any other options, Cheryl, reluctantly, was left to complete the rest of the trip unaccompanied. While staying alone in one of the accommodations in France, Cheryl was raped.

That news shattered my world. I did not know what to say. I felt lost and confused. It was as if a bomb had exploded in front of me and I was shell-shocked. But, instead of running away, the opposite happened. Gathering my thoughts and emotions I determined then and there that Cheryl and I would be together. We had already resolved, through all the waves of obstacles that kept coming against us, that we would not abandon each other, not now and not ever.

Standing By Cheryl

I decided to drop out of school to be next to Cheryl, to be there for her. Ironically, this issue caused me to feel closer to Cheryl than I had ever felt before. In other words, this crisis tightened our bond together, making it even more unbreakable.

Given Cheryl's condition, I was afraid that when her parents found out that they would step in and take her away from me. With everyone asleep at 2:00 am in the morning, I told her that we needed to run away immediately. We quietly gathered what we could and silently made our way to the car when Cheryl's brother woke up. He asked where we were going. We told him that we were running away to get married. He said, "Great!" Wanting to keep it a secret, we never told him that Cheryl was pregnant and how it happened.

As we drove south to Cincinnati, it suddenly dawned on me that a baby was going to be born, loading on us the responsibility to raise a child. It did not take long for me to realize we were not at all ready to become parents. I was nineteen and Cheryl was twenty-two. We had no job, no place to stay, no family or friends for support and no direction in life. I was terrified! I told Cheryl that it would be best for us to use adoption to place the baby in a good home. We both agreed that abortion was out of the question and that adoption was our only course of action.

"Dump her!"
(Dr. Luce)

On the way to Cincinnati we stopped at Miami University to get my belongings. A light snow was on the ground when we arrived at 6:30 in the morning. Just before dawn with the campus street lights still lit, I saw my French professor, Dr. Luce, walking to his office. Having been his students, both Cheryl and I knew and trusted Dr. Luce. I asked Cheryl to wait in the car as I was going to catch up with Dr. Luce to say goodbye and tell him that I would not be completing his course. Alone, I walked with him to his office. There I told him how Cheryl had been raped, was now pregnant and we were on our way to Cincinnati to get married. Dr. Luce turned to me frowning as he said, "Dump her. She is only trouble!" (I knew he was wrong.) Now, being hit by another wave of obstacle, I left his office with an even stronger determination to never abandon Cheryl. No matter what had happened in the past or what I had to deal with in the future, I would continue to stand by Cheryl.

Married

Leaving Oxford, Ohio we drove on to Cincinnati. Around 8:30 am we arrived at the courthouse. It was freezing cold as we huddled in the car waiting for the courthouse to open. Finally, the doors opened and we were the first ones to enter. We told the clerk we wanted to be married. The clerk asked Cheryl, "How old are you, young lady?" "Twenty-two," Cheryl replied. The clerk said, "Fine." Then the clerk turned to me and asked, "And how old are you, young man?" I responded, "Nineteen." Then came the next obstacle as the clerk said, "Oh, so you are nineteen. Well, here is the form for you. On this line your father must sign and on this line your mother must sign." I said, "But, they will never sign because I am Jewish, and she is not. What can we do?"

It was then that the clerk told us that we should cross over the Ohio River Bridge into Kentucky. She continued, "In Kentucky they don't care if you are eight years old and first cousins, they will marry you there." Before we left Cincinnati for Kentucky we managed to rent a small studio with just a pull-out couch for furniture. I called John "Randy" Roberts, my best friend, and Cheryl called Linda Aidala, her best friend, both from Miami University to come to be our best man and maid of honor. As loyal friends they agreed to meet us in Covington, Kentucky.

The sun light was glistening over the smooth water of the Ohio River as we crossed over into Covington. Once we arrived, we set off to buy wedding rings. There they were in the display window of a jewelry store, two matching gold wedding rings for $100. The problem was that I only had $100 which would have left me with nothing. So, I gave Cheryl $35 and put $65 in my pocket and then I went inside. I told the salesperson that I wanted the rings and only had $65. I put the $65 on the counter and pulled my pockets inside out to show that is all I had. I got the rings for $65. To this day I am still wearing that very same ring.

We then met up with Randy and Linda. I asked for directions and was told that the Justice of the Peace was Jack "Ducky" Mader who was at that time in a certain bar next to his office. Asking everyone to wait in the car, I went into the bar and found him. I told him that Cheryl and I wanted to get married, now. As he made his way over to his office I signaled for everyone to come. Ducky opened the door of his office and found his Bible and the marriage vows. We positioned ourselves directly in front of him, he opened the Bible, and recited the vows and paused for our responses. I was so anxious to be married that I hastily responded, "Yea, Yea, Yea." Concerned that I was taking the vows too lightly, Cheryl stopped me and said, "Listen to those vows carefully." Finally, Ducky Mader pronounced us husband and wife. Then he asked us for the rings which we put on each other. All that remained was for Ducky to fill out and sign the marriage license. Now, I had the precious document that proved that Cheryl and I were husband and wife. At last, we were married.

The Marriage Certificate

Back at the bare apartment, we celebrated by sitting on a blanket on the floor and feasting on Kentucky Fried Chicken and Bob's Big Boy Strawberry pie. I have never since had chicken and strawberry pie taste that good. That first wedding night was spent with Randy sleeping on the cold floor below my side of the pull-out couch and Linda sleeping on the cold floor below Cheryl's side of the pull-out couch.

Married life had begun. It was wonderful. I felt so complete and full of hope. Even in spite of all the obstacles we had faced, I was so optimistic that everything would be good from here on out. I had Cheryl and with Cheryl I knew I had all I needed in life.

Announcing the Marriage to Our Parents

We called Cheryl's parents to tell them that we were married. Immediately on the same day they drove down from Akron. As soon as they arrived, we informed them that Cheryl was pregnant and that the baby was going to be placed by adoption. We also made it clear to them that the baby was not mine, confirming that the time of conception was when she was in Europe. They were very angry with me because I had, without their permission (which they would not have given), taken their daughter and married her. Her father had a fifty-pound sack of potatoes when they arrived in our apartment which he handed to me when he left saying, "Here, you will need this." They opened the door and walked out into the cold winter, entered their car and drove away. We never saw them or talked with them until after the baby was born. To our knowledge they kept Cheryl's pregnancy a secret.

I called my mother to tell her that I was now married. She responded, "Oh, Tommy, that is divine. How do you like married life?" To which I replied, "Great, Mom. I should have done it years ago." She said, "Tommy, you are only nineteen years old!" I did not tell her that Cheryl was pregnant.

I called my father to also tell him that Cheryl was now my wife. In contrast, he exploded with great anger. He hung up the phone. Next, I received a phone call from his brother, my Uncle Jack, who was a surgeon in Miami, Florida. He told me that he was calling me on behalf of the family. He spoke to me calmly and presented a proposal. His proposal was for me to come to a place where there would be a table surrounded by family members. On the table would be a large sum of money. Without anyone saying a word, I was to take the money, get a quick divorce and forget about ever again marrying a Gentile and no one would ever mention this again. I replied, "Uncle Jack, that is pretty rough. Is there a Plan B?" He replied, "Yes, there is. Have a nice life." This meant that the family was saying goodbye to me forever. I chose Plan B. I chose Cheryl.

When I told Cheryl about that conversation Cheryl said, "Oh no! I married into a Jewish family and into a Jewish family I will be!" During the first year of our marriage, Cheryl set out to rebuild the relationship with my Jewish family. Later my father would sit at a dinner table with us and say that we were reconciled, explaining while looking at me, "Not because of you." Then pointing to Cheryl, "But, because of her."

Thanks to Cheryl, we were eventually accepted by my own Jewish family.

The Disillusionment
of the Relationship

I immediately got a job on the railroad for $1.00 per hour training to be a switchman. To save money we ate turkey tails that cost ten cents per pound. To this day I still like turkey tails.

I was glad we were married. Little did I expect that the rape would bring such a terror to our lives. The consequences of the rape were unimaginable. Clearly, Cheryl suffered from post-traumatic stress syndrome. Terrified in the dark she insisted on sleeping with the lights on at night. Still scared of being attacked, she would wake up in the middle of the night yelling, in cold sweats shaking. It was horrible for both us. It was those terrible symptoms that Cheryl endured that caused me to realize that I had no hope of being cleansed through my relationship with Cheryl. I tried to get Cheryl to agree to go to rape counseling. She would have nothing to do with it. She could not bear reliving through the counseling sessions the horrible time that terrified her. The rest of her life she chose the path that led her to hide the painful truth by denying that it ever happened. Her ultimate retaliation to the offender was to deny he ever existed. By not willing to face and deal with the ugly reality, she suffered immensely. (But, there was something I could not understand. It was a strength that kept Cheryl from drowning in despair during her darkest moments.)

It was now obvious to me that, through no fault of Cheryl's, she was no longer wholesome. She had become defiled. She was "damaged goods." Any hope I had of healing and recovery from her was shattered when she was violated and lost her innocence. All the help I had hoped to get from my relationship with her was now dead.

Where did that leave me? I still needed cleansing. I needed hope. I still needed to be free from the burden of the past. Where would I now turn? To whom would I go?

Cheryl was like a beautiful vase now shattered. I saw myself kneeling down on the floor trying to re-assemble that beautiful vase, the protected, sheltered symbol of innocence and purity. The task was impossible, too late. The clock could not be turned back.

Jewish Family Services

I had family in Cincinnati, but I did not contact them as we were in hiding to bury the past, to keep it a great secret. Wanting the baby to be raised in a Jewish home, I immediately contacted Jewish Family Services. They sent over to our apartment one of their staff members. Her name was Dottie. She told us that she would personally be responsible to find a good Jewish family to raise the baby.

What to tell Jewish Family Services surrounding Cheryl's pregnancy was one of the most crucial decisions we had to make. We were concerned that the chances of the baby being adopted lessened with the knowledge that Cheryl was raped. Therefore, without giving any further details about the conception, we simply told Jewish Family Services that the baby was from another man. Our goal was for the baby to be adopted. We especially wanted to make sure that we kept the painful fact of the rape a great secret and that Jewish Family Services would not have a written record of the rape that could be later exposed.

Prior to the baby's birth, Jewish Family Services informed us that they had located a good Jewish Family. This assured us that the baby would be taken care of. It was also vitally significant that Jewish Family Services promised us that our identities would never be revealed and that their files would always be sealed. Consequently, the child would never be able to track us down. This assurance secured for us what we essentially needed which was absolute secrecy. With this assurance, the past could finally be put behind us and we were now able to move on – so we thought. We were wrong. In the years ahead we constantly lived with the undercurrent of fear that the rape and pregnancy would be exposed.

Dr. Alberts & Jewish Hospital

With the adoption plan in place and the birth getting closer, we now focused our time on getting medical care for Cheryl. I had to find an obstetrician for Cheryl. When my mother separated from my father, she left Los Angeles for her parents' home in Cincinnati. At that time she was pregnant with me. Her obstetrician was Dr. Edward Alberts who delivered me at Cincinnati Jewish Hospital. With this link to me I contacted Dr. Alberts. Because Dr. Alberts did not know my father, Cheryl and I had the confidence that Dr. Alberts would not contact my father about the pregnancy. And since my mother, immediately following my birth, had moved back to Los Angeles, we had further confidence that Dr. Alberts would not reveal the secret to her either. For certain, both my Jewish parents would never know about the baby; our secret was secured. They never found out. With medical care and the adoption in place all that remained was for the baby to be born. We waited through the long winter months of pregnancy to be over. That winter was extremely cold for both of us.

The Search for Life

Even though Cheryl and I were together, I felt so alone in the crippling cold Cincinnati winter. I had no friends, no family and no one to confide in. That coldness penetrated into my soul with a piercing desolation. In addition, I was tormented by the disturbing memories and the guilt of my own sexual defilement which continued to haunt me. I was helplessly being carried away with strong oscillating feelings of hurt, blame, being robbed, violated, anger, guilt, hatred, remorse and sorrow. I could not get questions out of my mind: How could he...? How could her two friends...? How could God have allowed...? Relief was nowhere to be found. There was no comforting counselor. There was no distracting thought. There was no diverting preoccupation. There was no help.

What happened to Cheryl shattered my last hope in life. I desperately wanted to find hope and fulfillment in my life with her. But I came up empty. I felt as if I had grasped for the wind and opened my hand and found nothing.

I was desperately crying out for help. But, Cheryl, my only friend, was so deeply hurt and scared herself that she could not give me any relief. She could not, even if she wanted to, reach down to pull me out of the pit I was in. What was I to do? What I could not understand, however, as injured as Cheryl was, I saw something that I could not explain. While suffering from her own

42

inner pain and also completely alone, Cheryl was not being sucked down into the vortex of terror and sadness that I was plunging down into. I saw that she was being lifted up. I saw that she was being kept from falling into that lower level of the darkness of despair.

Clearly, the rape had left Cheryl with severe scars on her soul. She experienced nightmares, cold sweats and unreasonable paranoia. Yet, with each attack of terror Cheryl experienced a certain restoration, a peace which I did not experience. Every time she fell, she would rise again and again and again. In contrast, I fell deeper and deeper and deeper into a hole of depression, grief and sorrow. I felt that there was no relief for me. What Cheryl had I did not have. I wanted to know what she had.

Now, to my shame, I had to face the reality that Cheryl might have been right when she said that God exists. I painfully recalled my cavalier attitude when I announced to Cheryl that our home was absolutely going to be with "No God! No Bible! And No Church!" I now found myself crawling in agony to eat those words. From this lowest place my only recourse was to look up. Humbly, I now was asking questions. "God, are you there? God, are you there for me? God, can you give me what Cheryl has?"

The Cry to the Unknown

I saw my search for God as if my hand was reaching, stretching, and straining out into a darkness hoping that I would feel the responding hand of God. I was not searching for a religion as a substitute for God. I had plenty of it in Judaism. I had no interest in any form of an institutional God. I knew that no community of people with common beliefs could ever be a substitute for God. I did not even want Cheryl as a substitute for God (that already had not worked). Definitely, I was not looking for a God who was cold and distant. I wanted the God who was warm, close and personal, who understood and cared for me. My soul was reaching out to touch God, to hold God, to grab God, to cling to God. That is how I started my search for the God I did not know.

Through Cheryl I learned that this God I did not know could be found in the Bible. But I knew nothing about the Bible except that it was a big leather-bound book. Needing a copy, one day after work I secretly slipped into a store and bought one. To keep Cheryl from knowing that I was looking for God, I hid the Bible in my car. One thing was for sure, if I was going to find God I needed to find Him on my own, alone. To prevent her from knowing that I was searching for God, I told Cheryl that I had to work two hours extra every day and that I would be late coming home. Encouraged with the hope that I was finally going to find God I determined to spend those two hours per day in the Bible.

On the first day of my search for God, I sat at a table after work with that big Bible in front of me. Without opening it I just sat there staring at its cover. I had never read a book with that many pages before. With dyslexia I was never a reader. By the time I graduated from high school the largest book I had ever read had one hundred pages and that about killed me. But, in front of me now was a Book that had about two thousand pages. I thought of how hard it was going to be if I had to read through two thousand pages to find God. But, I knew I was at the end of my rope. It was my last chance in life to find relief. I had only one choice left. I had to search for God in the Bible.

Just as I was ready to open the Bible, I felt the need to pray. But I did not know how to pray. I had memorized many Jewish prayers that all began with, "Baruch Ata Adonai Eloheinu Melech Ha Olam" ("Blessed are you, Lord, our God, King of the Universe"). On cue I had recited those prayers many times without ever thinking that I was really talking to God. That, for me, was religion and now I needed reality. I did not want to insult God by repeating a memorized religious phrase. I was reaching out to God from a heart yearning to find Him as my friend.

So, instead of reciting a memorized Jewish prayer, I tried to formulate my own prayer from my heart. I started with the words, "O God." That was as far as I got. I felt I was not being honest because I really did not know if God existed. So, I modified my own prayer from the heart and said, "O God, if there is a God." I paused and thought, "If He is there what do I want?" I started again and said, "O God, if there is a God, help me." After that prayer I turned to the Bible.

Not knowing where to start, I opened it to the table of contents. Immediately I saw that the Bible was divided into two parts. One part was called "Old," and another part was called "New." I had no idea what "Old" and "New" meant. But, I saw that the "New" was about one third the size of the "Old." "Done deal," I concluded. I like the smaller "New," and I also wanted something "New" rather than something "Old."

The first book in the "New" section was a book called "Matthew." What became obvious to me was that this was a book about Jesus. This book was all about Jesus, Jesus, Jesus. That caused me to face a cross roads. I was taught that Jewish people have nothing to do with Jesus. As a Jewish person I was raised to shut the door to anything about Jesus. Now, I was reading a book that was all about Jesus. I had a difficult choice to make to either keep the door as it had been all my life, closed to Jesus or to open the door to learn who Jesus was and if Jesus could help me. That was a hard decision to open the door of my soul to a book that was all about Jesus. I was so desperate for help that I decided to open the door and look to Jesus for help.

As I read the book of "Matthew" I desperately tried to cling to the words I hoped would lead me to God. Written in a Shakespearean old English made me realize that it was going to be harder than I thought to find God. However, I was desperate for help. I was not going to give up. I pressed on day after day trying to understand what I was reading. But, I understood nothing. There was still no light in my darkness. My heart yearned to make sense out of the Bible. I felt as lost as ever.

Then it happened! In the fifteenth chapter I read the words of Jesus and felt that He was talking directly to me when He said:

> "For out of the heart proceed evil thoughts, murders, adulteries, fornications, thefts, false witness, blasphemies: These are the things which defile a man."
> (Matthew 15:19-20)

The two words, "adulteries and fornications," arrested me. In those two words I saw myself again going into that two-hour shower hoping to get clean from my own sexual sins that plagued me. I felt my own filthiness when Jesus said the words, "These are the things which defile a man." I also imagined my sexual sins spewing up from my own heart, making me so unclean within when Jesus said, "Out of the heart proceed..." I knew that what he was saying was true that the cause for my defilement came from inside of me. As I had always known, the cause of my defilement was not from outside of me, but from within. With his finger pointing right at me; I had no one else to blame. I could not blame my environment. I could not blame my upbringing. I could only blame myself. It was an, "I DID IT!" moment. The words of Jesus convicted me. His words were a painful declaration of fact. His words pinned me down and I knew it was the truth. I might as well have been in a court and seen the judge say to me: "Guilty as charged, condemned!" It hurt.

I closed the book and said to myself, "He knows me." He knows that my evil heart is oozing out defiling sexual thoughts. I had a heart issue. Since Jesus got the right diagnosis of my problem there was now a spark of hope. If Jesus knows my problem, then maybe He knows the solution. And if he can help me, I need to know: What? How? When?

With this hope that Jesus had the answer I was looking for, I pressed on. As I came to the end of the book of Matthew, I was shocked to read of how Jesus was hated, betrayed and tortured to die a slow, agonizing death on a cross. I felt so disappointed that the person I hoped could help me was now destroyed. Again I shut the book reaching out into the darkness for help to understand why. Why was the only person who was beginning to give me hope for relief from my defilement now so miserably destroyed? Then I remembered what my Jewish Uncle Pete, the former pharmacist at

Cincinnati Jewish Hospital, had said two years before.

Cheryl and I had joined his family for a Passover celebration at his home in Cincinnati. Uncle Pete had just finished reading the Haggadah book which recited how God had delivered the Jewish people from being exterminated in Egypt. My Aunt Mary was in the kitchen getting the cold chicken soup (it was always cold because it took so long to go through the Hagaddah). Uncle Pete was short and he wore glasses that looked like the bottom of coke bottles. He liked to chew on a cigar which irritated my Aunt Mary. As the dominant figure in the house, Aunt Mary practically told Uncle Pete what to think when he woke up every morning. In return, Uncle Pete loved to irritate Aunt Mary. At this particular Passover celebration while Aunt Mary was in the kitchen, Uncle Pete just blurted out, "Christians believe that Christ was the Passover Lamb!"

In our family just to say the name of Christ or Jesus was scandalous, unless to swear. So, when Uncle Pete announced that Christians believe that Christ was the Passover Lamb, it was shocking. Immediately my Aunt Mary shouted from the kitchen, "Pete, shut up!" And then Uncle Pete looked at me with glee in his eyes as if to say, "Wasn't that a great way to irritate her." Uncle Pete had no idea that when he said that Christians believed that Christ was the Passover Lamb that he planted a seed in my mind that would remain.

As I sat there two years later with the Bible closed in front of me, trying to process why Jesus was tortured to death, Uncle Pete's statement came back to me, "Christ was the Passover Lamb."

I wondered if just maybe Uncle Pete's sarcastic statement about Christ being the Passover Lamb was true. I turned to the Bible to find the history of the Passover, which, being Jewish, I heard year after year. I found the history in the book of Exodus, chapter 12. I read the account carefully. I realized that after sitting through so many Passover celebrations, that I really never understood the meaning of the Passover. I understood the Seder or the order of it all. But I never understood the "real" message of Passover. Somehow I had overlooked and never really grasped the centrality of the Passover lamb and the significance of the blood of the Passover lamb.

As I read Exodus, I saw the great tragedy of the Passover night which was that every first-born son in every family was going to die. It did not matter whether the family was Jewish or Egyptian, every first-born son was going to die. However, the Passover history in Exodus made it clear that God had a rescue plan in place to save the first-born. God's rescue plan was a lamb! It was clear that God's great rescue required each person, individually, to make their own personal identification, their own strong connection, their own determined link with a lamb. No lamb, no rescue. No lamb, no life for the first-born. All that was needed was just the lamb and only the lamb. Besides this, there was no other rescue for the first-born. God made it crystal clear that His great rescue required death, the death of the lamb. To display the lamb's death, its blood had to be put on the lintel and on the two side posts of the front door. No death of the lamb and no blood of the lamb on the front door of the house, means the first-born must die! There was no other requirement for them other than to **believe** that the blood of the lamb placed on the door was enough for God to spare the first-born.

The blood of that Passover lamb around the front door of the house was like an intervention between a God of judgment and a frightened and terrified family inside the house. Therefore, on that night the Passover lamb was killed and the blood was splashed over the top and on the two side posts of the front door of the house. With the blood on the two side posts and dripping down from the lintel of the front door, a shape of a cross emerged. Then, I read God's promise:

> "And the blood shall be to you for a token upon the houses where ye are: and when I see the blood, I will pass over you, and the plague shall not be upon you to destroy you, when I smite the land of Egypt." (Exodus 12:13)

I saw clearly that the angel of judgment and death would "pass over" or just skip every door with the blood of the lamb. All along as I read and thought about the Passover lamb and the death of Jesus it was Uncle Pete's words that kept resonating in my mind, "Christians believe that Christ was the Passover Lamb." I kept reading the New Testament until all at once, in one verse, it all crystalized for me. It was the words of John the Baptist who seeing Jesus for the first time said:

"Behold the Lamb of God, which taketh away the sin of the world." (John 1:29)

There it was! Summed up in one simple statement was my own personal rescue! It had now all fallen into place. In that one simple statement by Uncle Pete was the link between the relief I had been looking for from the torment of my defilement and Jesus, the Lamb of God. For me, Jesus had to become my Passover Lamb, the Lamb destined to die to take away my guilt and sins. For me, this was the truth I had been searching for. This was the "What" of my rescue. Now, I had to find the "How" and "When." How was I going to make Jesus my personal Passover Lamb to take away my sins? And "When" would this happen?

"Would I Still be Jewish?"

Being Jewish still defined me. Clinging to who I am, my identity was important to me. So, I wanted to know that if I made Jesus my personal Passover Lamb to take my sin away, would I no longer be Jewish? This was a dilemma for me. I had always been taught that people who were not Jewish were either Christians or Moslems, that a Jewish person could never be a Christian. Growing up, I believed that to be a Christian meant to no longer be Jewish. But, I really did not know what it meant to be a Christian. I did not know if the terms "Christian" and "Jewish" were mutually exclusive. I had not given much thought to this question.

In Cincinnati, during lunch at work I regularly ate with three non-Jewish co-workers. I knew that in the US the overwhelming majority of non-Jewish persons called themselves Christians. I knew my three co-workers were not Moslems, they must be Christians. So, to answer my question of what it meant to be a "Christian," I thought that my three co-workers would be a good place for me to find out. All my co-workers were married men. As I sat quietly and listened to them at lunch, I was shocked to hear them talk so freely with each other about their sexual adventures with their mistresses. Because my wife had been violated, faithfulness in marriage was very important to me. But, they had no shame as they talked about cheating on their wives. Since I considered them Christians, I wanted to know if it was OK for a

Christian to cheat on his wife. Does Jesus have any influence over a Christian's marital fidelity? The answers to those questions would tell me their relationship to Jesus Christ. I was going to find out.

One day as they began to talk about their adulterous sexual exploits, I realized that the time was perfect for me to find out what it meant to be a "Christian." Right in the middle of them talking about their extra-marital relationships, I announced, "You fellows need Jesus Christ." It did not matter to me that I did not understand what I was saying. I was trying to find out if being a Christian meant having Jesus Christ. Their response gave me the crystal clear answer. They were insulted by what I said. Immediately, I was excluded from the group. That was the last time I was invited to have lunch with them.

Their strong reaction told me that they did not have and they did not want to have Jesus Christ. Those "Christian" co-workers of mine made me understand that I can have Jesus Christ without becoming a "Christian." From their response, I learned that a person could be a Christian and not have Jesus Christ or, expressed differently, I learned that a person could have Jesus Christ and not be called a Christian. To be a Christian then has nothing to do with having Jesus Christ. To me, this confirmed that to take Jesus Christ as my Passover Lamb did not make me a Christian and did not stop me from being Jewish. In short, I can have Jesus Christ and still remain Jewish.

The Birth

It was April. The time for Cheryl to give birth had come. We went to Cincinnati Jewish Hospital where Cheryl was put under general anesthesia.

Cincinnati Jewish Hospital

The baby was born. Cheryl was returned to her room still under sedation. I was waiting outside Cheryl's room when I saw Dr. Alberts holding the baby heading towards Cheryl's room. Instantly, I blocked Dr. Alberts from entering Cheryl's room. "No, Cheryl is not to see the baby," I told Dr. Alberts. He turned back and Cheryl never saw the baby.

The hospital called me to the nursery and informed me that my name would appear on the birth certificate as the father and Cheryl's as the mother. Then the nurse explained to me that as the father of record on the birth certificate that it was now my responsibility to name the baby. I wanted the baby to be raised Jewish so I told the nurse that her name was to be Judith.

A New Beginning

We left the hospital and the sun hit my face, it felt warm. So opened the next new chapter of our married life.

Spring had finally arrived. The winter had drained us emotionally and now the sunshine had broken through the clouds and flowers were pushing out the dark and gloom of winter. With the winter past we felt as though we had come to the spring of our married life together. Our lives then moved into the recovery period. Cheryl got a job with Proctor and Gamble opening envelopes with coupons and I already had a job at Hilton Davis in a chemical pilot plant. Life goes on.

California Before Us
Ohio Behind Us

It was now September and we had emerged from our hibernation in Cincinnati. We had managed to save $1500 and we felt rich. We returned to the home of Cheryl's parents in Akron where no one spoke a word about a baby. Late one evening we finished packing our stuff in the car and the next morning said our goodbyes to Cheryl's parents and drove away. San Diego was in our sights as I hoped to finish my biochemistry undergraduate studies at the University of California at San Diego. With the windows rolled down we were finally on the road to California and we had such a feeling of relief. The great secret of the rape and pregnancy was secure. We both had hoped that we could finally put the whole terrible experiences of the past behind us as we drove from Ohio to California.

As I looked in the rear view mirror, everything got smaller and smaller. I thought that the only relatives that knew the great secret were getting smaller and smaller. All the disturbing reminders and memories of the past with the rape and the subsequent birth of the baby and the adoption process were all now behind us as we made our way across the country.

Found at Last

It was now time for me to tell my wife that I needed God. I did not know how to express this new desire, so I just told her that I was becoming "religious." Cheryl said nothing as tears began to roll down her face. I told her that I did not want to become a "Christian" and had no desire to attend "Church." I emphasized that I was Jewish and that I needed to return to the Jewish synagogue. I hoped that in the synagogue my search for God would end.

When we arrived in San Diego, I got a newspaper and found the largest reformed Jewish temple in San Diego, Temple Beth El. I called the rabbi on the phone. I started by telling him that I had been reading what Moses wrote in the book of Exodus about the Passover. As soon as I mentioned Moses, the rabbi interrupted me and told me that he did not believe that there really was a literal person named Moses. He told me that he believed that the books of Moses were written by a series of writers using the pen name of Moses. I could not believe what I was hearing.

To me, the rabbi was saying that the Passover did not really happen. That cut across what I believed all my life. If what the rabbi was saying was true, then the origin of the whole Jewish nation and the God of the Jews as the one and only true God was not as the Bible reported.

What that rabbi said caused me to remember a statement by another rabbi when I was at a Junior High School retreat, the Jewish Camp Hess Kramer in Malibu. At that time, gathered around a campfire, we were invited to ask the rabbi any question. I spoke up and asked the rabbi the classic Jewish troubling question, "Where was God during the holocaust?" Without even thinking the rabbi quickly responded, "You must understand that God is very busy and that was a time when God was preoccupied." As a twelve-year old, that response extinguished any potential interest I might have had in God. In my search now for God, I was not interested to find a God not involved in the Passover. I was not interested in finding a God who was preoccupied and too busy. So, when that rabbi told me that he did not think that Moses was a real person, I said on the phone, "I'm sorry. I think I dialed the wrong number" and I hung up the phone. Where to next?

With the reformed synagogue crossed off the list, I then decided to go to the orthodox synagogue and speak to a rabbi. Again, back to the newspaper, I found an orthodox Jewish synagogue, Temple Tifereth. I went to the Friday night service. I listened carefully to the rabbi's message looking for something the rabbi said that would help me find God. During the message I realized, as I looked around, that I was the only one glued to the rabbi's words. Most of the people were visiting with one another. I started to think that I had come to a social club and not a place to find God.

I was not going to leave without trying to find God. Right after the rabbi's message, I went to speak to the rabbi alone. I started by asking, "Rabbi, I don't know, but I think Jesus may have been the Messiah." I was not entirely surprised, when the rabbi pulled his shoulders back, glared at me and declared, "This is the first time and this is the last time you will ever say that name again!" I felt so low that I could sit on a dime and swing my legs. I wanted an explanation, instead I got a strong rebuke for a response. For me it was not unexpected when the rabbi despised the name of Jesus. Being Jewish I had been raised with a strong prejudice against that name.

For me, the roads to Jesus as the lamb of God through the reformed and orthodox Judaism were blocked. So, it was back again to the newspaper to find where I could go for answers. I needed to find God! It was then that I found that there was an Emmanuel Baptist Church that was going to show a movie on Israel entitled "His Land." The name of that church fascinated me because that was the same name of the Jewish synagogue I attended as a boy, Temple Emmanuel in Beverly Hills. I was afraid because it was a church. What if I went to this church and was identified as Jewish and accused of killing their god?

I tried to conceal the fact that I was Jewish as I slowly entered the auditorium. I took my seat at the rear of the room next to the exit door so I could have a fast get-away before anyone noticed I was there. When the movie finished I stood up to make a quick exit when I felt a hand on my shoulder. As I turned around to see who it was, I saw an elderly lady who said, "You are Jewish?" Just as I feared, I responded, "What? Do I have the map of Jerusalem on my face? Why would you say that?" She did not want me to be afraid as she told me that she did not hate the Jews and that the pastor's grandmother was Jewish.

When she saw that I was relieved, she introduced me to another Jewish person who was a member of the church, Eve Rule. Eve introduced me to the pastor, Ray Hahn. The pastor and I agreed to meet the next day. At the meeting, I explained to the pastor that I had been reading what Moses wrote in the Book of Exodus about the Passover lamb. I told him what I found in the New Testament when John the Baptist described Jesus as the Passover Lamb of God that takes sin away. At that point the pastor interrupted me and said, "I do not know where you stand with Jesus. You are telling me that you believe many things in the Bible, But, have you ever received Jesus as your personal God and Savior?" I told him that I had no idea what he was saying when he talked about "receiving Jesus." But, I wanted to know because I wanted to know if this "receiving Jesus" was finally going to be the answer to my question of "how" I could make Jesus my personal Passover Lamb to take my sin away.

I asked him how you do that, how does a person receive Jesus as God and Savior. He wanted to make clear to me the difference between believing and receiving. He said that it was like the difference between believing that he was offering me the gift of a book and me actually reaching out my hand and taking the book to myself. Just believing that the book was being offered to me was not the same as actually receiving the book. As long as the book remained in his hand and out of my hand, I had not received the book even though I believed that the book was being offered to me. To receive the book, I had to reach my hand out, and take it to make it mine. From that example I understood what was meant by "receiving Jesus" which the pastor showed me in the book of John:

> "But as many as **received** him, to them gave he power (authority) to become the sons of God, even to them that **believe** on his name." (John 1:12)

That "receiving Jesus" sounded like what I was looking for, the "how" I could make Jesus my personal Passover Lamb to take my sin away. I was excited to think that I had also come to the "when" I could make Jesus my Passover Lamb to take my sin away. I wanted to do that now. I was in. I told the pastor that I wanted to receive Jesus as my God and Savior. He told me that all I needed to do was to pray to God.

First, I had to tell God that I am a sinner. I looked at the pastor and thought, "The pastor does not know me, but if he did, he would know from my past just how easy it is for me to tell God that I am a sinner." So, no problem with me telling God that I am a sinner.

Second, I had to tell God that I believed the Bible's account that God became a man named Jesus to be punished on the Cross for all the sins I had done. Well, I was already down the road of believing the Bible. I just had to believe that Jesus as God had become a man and died for me. The pastor showed me:

"Christ died for our sins."
(I Corinthians 15:3)

That squared with what I had been reading for myself in the Bible and what Uncle Pete had said, that Christ was the Passover Lamb.

Finally, I had to take my own personal step forward to cross over from just believing to actually receiving. That step forward of crossing over was very real to me because it was also a step forward of crossing over through all of the barriers of prejudice against the name and person of Jesus that I as a Jewish person had been taught. That step forward was real to me as I saw myself casting down all my weapons of resistance and rebellion against God as Jesus. That step forward was real to me as I no longer saw myself as a Jewish person or any other person other than just Tom who was coming to God as a dirty rotten sinner. That step forward was not me crossing a line into Christianity. That step forward was not me becoming a Christian. That step forward was not me coming to a religion. That step was me coming to the Lord Jesus Christ. That step forward from believing to receiving Jesus was like the act of reaching out my hand to take the gift and make the gift mine. I made my decision to take the critical step where I would tell God that I personally wanted to open my heart and receive Jesus as my God and personal Passover Lamb. As a Jewish person the most difficult aspect of this stepping over the line was to cast off my ingrained prejudice against Jesus being God. That was an ingrained prejudice that I had all my life. But, I had come to this point in my life. Now, it would be with this simple prayer that I would actually open my heart to receive Jesus as my God and Passover Lamb.

The pastor told me that he would help me by having me repeat after him a childlike prayer. I tried as best I could to pray from my heart the words of the simple prayer of: "Lord Jesus, I am a sinner. I believe you are God and became a man and died for my sins. Please forgive me of my sins. Come into my heart to be my God and Savior. Amen."

As soon as I raised my head from that prayer I felt two great changes. The first change was that I finally knew I belonged. No longer did I feel lost! Finally, Jesus found me!

"The Son of man is come to seek and to save that which was lost." (Luke 19:10)

Cleansed at Last

The second change after that prayer was that I also knew that finally I was cleansed. Clean at last! In Europe, I was sexually defiled. That feeling of being dirty inside tormented me for years. Now, what I could not get from a two-hour shower in Switzerland or a relationship with Cheryl, was instantly accomplished when I received Jesus as God into my heart. It was all so simple. I did not have to obey a set of laws for what not to do on the Sabbath. I did not have to obey a set of Kosher laws for what to not eat. To be cleansed all I had to do was just believe and receive Jesus Christ as my Passover Lamb. I felt like a person at that first Passover night in Exodus who just had to believe God when God made it so simple that all that was needed to spare the first-born from death was the blood of the lamb on the door. All I needed for cleansing and to be spared from judgment was to believe God that receiving Jesus would cleanse me and spare me from judgment. I was so happy that I felt I could sing: "Once I was defiled, now I am clean! Once I was lost, now I belong!"

How amazing that only my simple prayer, prayed as best I could, to receive Jesus into my heart, would finally bring me that cleansing fountain I looked for:

> "In that day there shall be a fountain opened to the house of David and to the inhabitants of Jerusalem for sin and for uncleanness." (Zechariah 13:1)

That cleansing fountain came to me from the love of Jesus who gave Himself to be my Passover Lamb:

"Jesus Christ...loved us, and washed us from our sins in his own blood." (Revelation 1:5)

Forgiven to Forgive

What a day that was for me in September 1970 when my new life began! That was the day when guilt and shame lost its voice to terrify me. That was the day when I knew that I had found the friend I was looking for. When I received Jesus into my heart God became my friend. When I received Jesus into my heart the Bible became the voice of God, my friend. I cherished the words of the Bible that said that none of my sins would ever stand between me and God:

> "For thou hast cast all my sins behind thy back." (Isaiah 38:17)

> "I will forgive their iniquity, and I will remember their sin no more." (Jeremiah 31:34)

> "As far as the east is from the west, so far hath he removed our transgressions from us." (Psalm 103:12)

> "Thou wilt cast all their sins into the depths of the sea." (Micah 7:19)

I no longer feared death. Jesus had died for my sins and became my Passover Lamb that spared me from the judgment for my sins. On that day in September 1970 I not only believed that Jesus Christ was God, I received into my heart Jesus Christ as God and I knew that I was forgiven. But,

I still faced a dilemma. There was one issue that still plagued me. If God had forgiven me, could I continue to carry bitterness against the man who raped Cheryl? What troubled me was the question, "If God had forgiven me, could I continue in life to not forgive the man who attacked Cheryl?" I saw I could no longer continue to hate that man and wish he was dead. I saw I could no longer want revenge. I HAD TO FORGIVE HIM! But, how was I going to fully forgive that man whose name I did not even know. I asked God for the way for me to forgive that man. That was when I started to think of my past and my own sexual defilements and how much God had forgiven me. As I looked at my past I was able to walk in the shoes of the man who sexually attacked Cheryl. As I looked at my past I remembered how condemned I was and I just could no longer condemn that man. I saw clearly that I was just as guilty in my heart of what I blamed that man for. I was no better than he. I saw how much God had forgiven me. That is what enabled me to forgive him. And I did. I thought about the relief I got from my sins when I received Jesus into my heart as God, my Passover Lamb. That led me to pray for that man to receive Jesus as I did and get relief from his sins.

At last, on that September day, my broken life of being lost and defiled was rebuilt into a life of being found and cleansed. It all happened when I prayed to Jesus and received Him as my God and my Passover Lamb. Now, I call Him the Lord Jesus Christ and when I do I mean that Jesus is God.

The Rebuilt Purpose in Life

I had found God and God had found me. But I could not tell my story of the "great rescue" while the "great secret" remained which was Cheryl's rape and pregnancy.

I got accepted into the University of California at San Diego. Cheryl got a job as a secretary and put me through school. I graduated with an undergraduate degree in Biochemistry. I worked for four years in medical research.

My work was demanding. I was putting in long hours and I missed being with Cheryl. So, in 1976 with just $130, I started the biotech company, Scantibodies Laboratory where I still can be reached today at tom.cantor@scantibodies. com. My goal was to work in the garage of my home to be close to Cheryl. Later, we moved to a ranch in Lakeside, California, where our family, now with the addition of three sons, lived for ten years as we continued to build the business.

At that ranch we assembled 300 goats to immunize for the production of antibodies for diagnostic tests. Work was twenty-four hours a day because the goats needed round the clock care. It was hard work.

Our three sons were put to work in our home-based business. Our home was like a Grand Central Station. To educate our boys, my wife home-schooled them for fourteen years. Our business slowly grew to forty-eight employees working in our home twenty-four hours a day. We had to take care of the business, those were the years of making the business first priority, "business first." This meant I was taking care of "my business" first!

In the year 2002, Quest Diagnostics sued Scantibodies Laboratory for patent infringement. I asked our defense attorneys how much it was going to cost us to defend ourselves in court. They told us $2-3 million (it actually cost us $8 million.) At this stage of growing the business, we had begun to invest in a new production facility in Tecate, Mexico and we were relying on the bank to finance $8 million for that building. We only had $1 million in the bank. We were $15 million short to cover the $8 million in legal fees and the $8 million construction fees in Tecate. The clincher was that the bank was not interested in financing a company being sued. The trial lasted five years. We eventually won. During the time of the trial, we were not focused on the business; the lawsuit consumed us as it was a matter of survival. Then, a miracle happened! At the time of the lawsuit, we had been in business for about 25 years with only $1 million in the bank. During those five years of court trial, no one was minding the shop. We should have gone bankrupt. But, the opposite happened. During those five years $15 million of profits were generated from the business. It was like $15 million just rained down on us. With that $15 million in profits we had enough to pay for the legal fees and the new construction in Tecate. We never went into debt then, or ever since.

That $15 million in unexpected profit was too much for me to not talk to God about, I said to God, "God, You just took care of the business." Then, a thought came to me, a thought that would become my life principle. It was like God was saying to me, "Yes, I did take care of your business. You take care of my business and I will take care of your business." I told God, "Deal!" I started to take care of God's business and never looked back again on just taking care of my business. Before that, my focus was on money. I used to look at suppliers and ask, "How can I buy at a lower cost?" I used to look at customers and ask, "How can I sell at a higher price?" But, now I look at people and ask the question, "Does he have Jesus as his personal Passover Lamb or not?" If he does not then I try to encourage him to take Jesus as his Personal Passover Lamb. If he does then I try to encourage him in his walk with God.

But, to help people meant that I needed to tell people how God helped me and that meant that I needed to tell people what the issue was that God helped me get through. But, I could not because I was hiding the issue in a "great secret" of the rape and pregnancy of Cheryl. I could not be completely transparent. I could not be real. Hiding this "great secret" got in the way of me helping others by telling what God saved me from. Then, once day it all changed!

23andMe and the Great Reveal

In 2019 it happened!

Our youngest son decided to have his personal genetic makeup tested by 23andMe. He was informed that he had a half-sister and received her contact information and her photograph.

He called me and asked what it meant. I immediately met with my three sons separately, and explained that their mother had been raped and became pregnant and that we had decided that adoption, not abortion, was the only course of action. Next, I further explained to them that the real history of what drove me to make Jesus my personal Passover Lamb was the rape and pregnancy of my wife, their mother. My sons were the first ones to know my real life history. It felt so good to tell them the whole history and be transparent and real. The living proof of my life history was the reality that they did have a half-sister.

Even though I had not planned on this "great reveal," yet, I was so thankful that after 50 years of cover-up, escape and denial, I could now come out of the darkness of secrecy and into the light of transparency. I could finally tell what God rescued me from when He took my broken life and rebuilt it centered in the Lord Jesus Christ. I am now free to tell the whole truth of how God rescued me!

Defiled to be Cleansed

My life is a history of being lost and defiled. I was lost coming from a broken home. I was lost from education, being expelled from schools. I was lost from a close relationship with my parents through their multiple marriages. My morality was lost when I was sexually defiled in Europe. Finally, I was lost and without hope when Cheryl was raped.

The night I went into the Miami University Library, I was looking for a person different from me. I was looking for a person who was pure, wholesome and innocent. I had hoped that through a relationship with her that, finally, I could belong to a person who would cleanse me from my own impurity, immorality and defilement. Later I looked forward to being married together with her where her purity, wholesomeness and innocence could somehow change me.

But, when Cheryl told me that she had been raped and was pregnant I was crushed. Cheryl was no longer pure, wholesome and innocent. The rape of Cheryl pulled the rug out from under me. Cheryl could no longer be my path to cleansing. I had looked up to her to make me whole. I had made her an idol placing her on a pedestal. She would be my savior lifting me from my own uncleanness, guilt and shame. My idol was shattered when from her lips I learned that she had been robbed of her purity and was pregnant. Impure, she was no longer better than I. No longer could she rescue me from my own impurity.

What was worse about the rape of Cheryl and the pregnancy was that it forced me to have to be reminded of my own sexual defilement. Her pregnancy was a glaring reminder of my own acts and defilements.

When Cheryl told me that she had been sexually violated and was pregnant I nose-dived into a downward spiral. Finally, it was in that eighth month of Cheryl's pregnancy, in the dead of that winter in Cincinnati that I hit rock bottom. I was so desperate for help. With nowhere else to turn to, I reached out for God, the God of the Passover Lamb. It was in that state of brokenness that I found in the Bible hope from who Jesus really is.

It was in 1970 when I made the most important decision in my life. In that decision I saw myself as bending below the truth that Jesus is God:

> "Jesus said unto them, Verily, verily, I say unto you, Before Abraham was, I am." (John 8:58)

I wanted to hear Him speak to me through the Bible. I wanted Him to be my guide though life. That was the process of Him rebuilding my life. I am no longer haunted by memories of my past and I am no longer fearful of the future. I have been lifted out of the muck of guilt, shame and despair. I have been set firmly on a rock: The Lord Jesus Christ.

> "He brought me up also out of an horrible pit, out of the miry clay, and set my feet upon a rock, and established my goings." (Psalm 40:2)

Part 2: Rebuilt

You now know how I was lost and defiled and broken. You also now know how I was rebuilt when I was found and cleansed after I received the Lord Jesus Christ into my heart as my Passover Lamb and God. In being rebuilt, God has given me my life motto: "You take care of my business and I will take care of your business." God's business is people. Here are two true accounts to illustrate what it means for me to take care of God's business.

Simon Wasserman

The first true account is about Simon Wasserman whose life has inspired me to become like him. "Taking care of God's business" for me means that I have become a Simon Wasserman: A man who took great risks to save people.

I have dear friends in Jerusalem named Avi and Tami. Tami's father's name was Simon Wasserman. Simon Wasserman was born into a Jewish home in Berlin, Germany, in 1910. Simon's father was a Schocket (or Jewish slaughterer) just like my grandfather was in Petersburg, Virginia. Simon had a brother and two sisters and the family enjoyed a pleasant, happy Jewish life in Berlin.

Berlin at that time was one of the great world centers for the arts, music, cabaret, literature, business and science. It was a beautiful city of majestic buildings with parks, rivers, lakes and tree-lined avenues like "Unter Den Linden Strasse."

Life for the Wasserman family was very comfortable as Simon's father enjoyed a respected position in the thriving Jewish community of Berlin. Simon was tall and with his blonde hair and blue eyes he did not look Jewish. As Simon was growing up he not only had Jewish friends, but he also had German friends.

Then, in 1930 when Simon was twenty years old, Simon's sister who had married a Jewish Zionist shocked the family with her announcement that she and her husband were moving to Palestine. At that time, moving from the highly civilized city of Berlin to the undeveloped and dangerous territory of Palestine was strange and only for the most bizarre nonconformists.

Meanwhile, Simon had begun to watch carefully a new rising politician named Adolf Hitler. Simon read Hitler's book "Mein Kampf" and was aware of Hitler's anti-Semitic intentions. Simon became convinced that Adolf Hitler was very dangerous for the Jewish people. After careful consideration Simon decided that he would also leave Germany and join his sister and her husband in Palestine.

So, in 1932, Simon applied to the British government for permission to immigrate to Palestine. The British government informed Simon that they had enough Jews in Palestine and that no more Jews were being given permission to immigrate there. However, there was a new technology of elevators in Palestine and there was a shortage of elevator technicians. This meant that if a Jew was an elevator technician, he would be given permission to immigrate to Palestine.

So, in 1932, Simon Wasserman enrolled in a one-year elevator technician course at the Berlin Technical Institute. Finally, in 1933, with his elevator technician certificate in hand, Simon Wasserman was given permission by the British government to immigrate to Palestine. (1933 was also the year that Hitler became chancellor and gained power over Germany.)

In Palestine, life was rewarding for Simon, as Jews were filled with the vision of creating a homeland. Meanwhile Tami's mother was beautiful and had come from Latvia also with the intention to immigrate into Palestine. But, at the border the British took a large sum of money from her and told her to leave the country in three months or forfeit the money and be hunted down as an illegal alien. Desperate to stay, Tami's mother found an old Yemenite Jew who agreed to marry her for convenience so she could stay in the country.

One day on the beach in Tel Aviv, Simon met Tami's mother and they fell in love. The couple went to the old Yemenite Jew to ask for a divorce and the old Yemenite Jew refused, explaining that he had fallen in love with Tami. Finally, they convinced him to give the divorce and Tami's father and mother were married. Together the young, happy couple built their life in the Jewish homeland. But they, like all Jews, watched carefully the troubling clouds of anti-Semitism as Hitler's goal of exterminating Jews progressed unstopped.

In November of 1938 came the horrible "crystal night" when all throughout Germany, store windows of Jewish shops were broken, Jewish houses and apartments were destroyed, and synagogues were demolished and set on fire. Many Jews were arrested, some were beaten, and some were even killed.

By 1939, all the world knew that Jews in Germany were being taken from their homes in the middle of the night and never seen again. There were terrifying eye witness reports of mass exterminations of Jews in horrible camps.

In that same year (1939) Simon Wasserman received a letter from Berlin. When he opened the letter, he was surprised to see that it came from one of his former German friends. The letter read:

"My Dear Simon, I have risen to a very high position in the Gestapo and SS and I am now looking at a list of Jews to be murdered. Your mother, father, sister and brother are on the list. Simon, because you are my dear friend, I am going to stick my neck out for you and your family. The second page of this letter is a two-week pass. With this pass you will be able to come back into Germany, back to Berlin and back to your home. With this pass you will be allowed to leave Germany and to take with you your father, mother, sister and brother in order to save them alive."

Simon showed the letter to his wife and friends who told him that he was out of his mind if he even considered going back to Germany. They reasoned with him that it was a trap and that when he arrived in Germany, the pass would be taken away from him. Then what would he be? He would be just another Jew on his way to the death camps. They told Simon that he could not trust a person who sold his soul to Hitler's Gestapo and SS Squad, as they were the very ones destroying the Jews. They pleaded with Simon not to walk into the "mouth of the lion."

Simon struggled with these thoughts, but the hopeless plight of his family was too great a pull on his heart. Simon had decided that cost what it would, he had no choice. Simon concluded that he would never be able to live with himself if he did not go to his family's rescue. He thought that if he died trying to save his family, he would die meeting the same end as his family in Berlin. He only knew that he must try to rescue them.

Simon set off from Palestine for Germany. When he entered Germany, he was shocked to see how his fellow Jews were treated as despised animals. The pass protected Simon as he was allowed to return to his family's home. When he arrived, he showed his family the letter and explained the reason for his coming. What do you suppose that his family told him? They said, "Simon, we are Germans! Palestine? Simon, are you out of your mind? It is dangerous in Palestine.

There are Arabs in Palestine, bullets, plus it's dirty. Look at how beautiful it is here in Berlin! You want us to leave the beauty of this city for the sand, dust, dirt, swamps and malaria of Palestine? Simon, look at the beauty of our house and all our possessions! You want us to leave all of this? The letter is a trap to get us to abandon our possessions to your so-called 'friend' who is really just a thief. To leave all of our possessions is a terrible price to pay. Don't speak such foolishness, Simon – we are Germans."

Simon again showed them the letter and they reiterated that it was only a trick to confiscate their nice home and possessions. Simon told them of the reports of concentration camps and mass exterminations and they replied with "Rumors, Simon, did you see these camps yourself? Did you see any of these mass exterminations? We are talking about Germany, the highest civilization in the world. Don't talk such nonsense."

Simon pleaded with them to consider Adolf Hitler to which they replied, "Hitler? He's a mad man. He will be assassinated. He will be overthrown or voted out of office. He is a temporary problem." Simon pleaded with his family for two weeks and was finally forced to leave Germany empty-handed. All of his family were murdered.

I have been broken to be rebuilt as a Simon Wasserman to see others saved, cost what it will.

Larry Rust

The second true account is about Larry Rust. "Taking care of God's business" for me means that I have vowed to never let what happened to Larry Rust ever occur again on my watch.

Larry Rust was a neighbor at the ranch whose story illustrates the most important need in life: The need to not delay the decision to make Jesus the personal Passover Lamb and God:

"Behold, now is the accepted time; behold, now is the day of salvation."
(2 Corinthians 6:2)

Larry Rust was a retired naval officer and we were good friends. I had tried numerous times to talk to Larry about God. He repeatedly rebuffed me. I gave up trying to talk to Larry about God. But, then Larry got prostate cancer.

While he was in Navy Hospital in Balboa Park in San Diego I decided to go visit Larry. I made my way to the cancer floor which was in the basement of the hospital. I had a big, black Bible in my hand. As soon as I appeared in the door Larry started to yell at me, "No! No God! No Bible! Get out of here!" It was a terrible scene and I just said, "OK, Larry. OK. I am going." I decided to give Larry a few days to cool off before I tried to visit Larry again without my Bible.

Later I returned to the cancer floor and Larry was not in his room. So, I went to the nurse and said, "Where is Larry?" The nurse looked at me with squinted eyes and said, "And who wants to know?" I thought the way she asked me was strange. I replied, "Tom." The nurse said to me, "Oh, so you are Tom." I said, "Yea." The nurse then said to me, "Well, let me tell you something, Mr. Tom. Larry Rust died last night. But, all through the night Larry was screaming, 'Tom, Tom. Where is Tom? Bring Tom. Bring Tom.'"

I just turned away. I vowed to never give up talking to people about the greatest treasure one can find in life and the need for them to make Him their personal Passover Lamb.